Camilo Andres Cardozo León

Public management with the application of artificial intelligence

Camilo Andres Cardozo León

Public management with the application of artificial intelligence

A perspective of improvement in citizen attention in the district mobility secretary's office

ScienciaScripts

Imprint

Cover image: www.ingimage.com

This book is a translation from the original published under ISBN 978-613-9-46840-9.

Publisher:
Sciencia Scripts
is a trademark of
Dodo Books Indian Ocean Ltd. and OmniScriptum S.R.L publishing group

120 High Road, East Finchley, London, N2 9ED, United Kingdom
Str. Armeneasca 28/1, office 1, Chisinau MD-2012, Republic of Moldova, Europe
Managing Directors: Ieva Konstantinova, Victoria Ursu
info@omniscriptum.com

Printed at: see last page
ISBN: 978-620-8-50876-0

REFORMING PUBLIC MANAGEMENT WITH THE APPLICATION OF ARTIFICIAL INTELLIGENCE: A PERSPECTIVE FOR IMPROVING CITIZEN SERVICES IN THE DISTRICT MOBILITY SECRETARIAT

SUMMARY

The object of study, in this case, will be focused on understanding technology and the relationship with society, which was projected by CONPES document in 2019 that opens the way to face the reality in a country where technology does not reach all corners and the waiting time to advance a procedure is too high compared to our neighbours, and for which it is valid to ask

How can AI be used as an aid tool to reduce the waiting time in the daily procedures of citizens, especially in the District Secretariat of Mobility?

As a thesis it is outlined that there is an anti-formalist reading, which makes visible a conflict of interests between the administration and the administered. The above to conclude that with the help of artificial intelligence and algorithms we can speed up the procedures for people who are worn out in terms of time with automated tools.

Key words:Artificial intelligence, public administration, managed, technology, customer care citizen.

TABLE OF CONTENTS

INTRODUCTION

Artificial intelligence (AI) is becoming a key tool for public administrations to support the changing dynamics of society. The application of AI in public administration can improve efficiency, reducing procedures, costs, time, optimising the quality of public services, and providing a better service to citizens.

AI can be used in Mobility secretariat, such as human talent management, public safety, education, customer service and decision making.

AI techniques to be used in public administration include automation of patterns or frequently asked questions, constant learning, data warehousing, insight from operating systems and cybernetics.

However, there are also misgivings related to the application of AI in public administration, such as the handling of information, which in some cases is confidential, as well as the correctness of the information provided to the user.

In sum, the reform of artificial intelligence in public administration needs to be linked as a valuable instrument to improve efficiency and quality of user care, but it is important to address the challenges and concerns associated with its implementation in a committed manner.

1. JUSTIFICATION OF THE CHOSEN THEME

Artificial intelligence (AI) shows us an immutable evolution that has experienced a growth over the days, and is becoming an important link in our daily lives. From automatic responses with From the support of bots, to decision making and process classification, AI is the present and future, showing us how to facilitate social dynamics with technology. The main justification for choosing AI as a research topic is that it has a huge impact on humanity, time and culture and is growing agilely. At the same time, AI presents many ethical and trust challenges that need to be addressed as the technology progresses. For example, there are concerns about personal data or proprietary public information, suspicion with algorithms, the impact that automation brings on the labour market, the liability of taking autonomous systems and the cyber-attacks it may suffer. Therefore, it is crucial to research and understand AI in depth in order to be better equipped to address these challenges and make the most of the opportunities offered by the technology. Furthermore, AI is a multidisciplinary field that encompasses different fields such as systems, mathematics, robotics, economics and others, making it a fascinating and enriching topic to explore from a variety of perspectives.

1.1. Problem and purpose of the work

The problem lies in the fact that these mechanisms (technological support), in Latin America, specifically in Colombia, are obsolete in their functioning to optimise, store and reduce the time required for personal procedures in public administrations, due to the fact that we have a technological backwardness with respect to first countries, in addition to possible failures in the algorithms that may arise in the implementation.

1.2. General and specific objectives

- General objective

The general objective is to implement artificial intelligence (AI) in the public sector, with a focus on improving citizen attention, creating a tool that allows to classify by subject the different problems that afflict citizens, facilitating the time that a person spends in a procedure before a notary or a claim in any state entity, mainly in the Ministry of Mobility where I worked for approximately two years, I observed how people arrived before 7:00 am, to make a line of a block and a half, when entering they were given a turn that was not linked to any program was manual voice to voice, depending on the speed of the officials inside the modules, to be able to serve them, they finished their diligence in the afternoon, The process basically consists of obtaining an administrative act that guarantees the removal of the vehicle or motorbike from the yards (the place where the means of transport is kept for failing to comply with certain traffic regulations). For this reason, it is feasible to implement a tool that coordinates by traffic offences and complexity of the matter via web with bank type security questions that only the owner knows to avoid fraud in the filling out, and allows to grant permission to remove the vehicle from the place where it is kept.

In Colombia this type of complexities does not only happen in the Secretary of Mobility, it also happens in the vast majority of entities where a procedure is carried out, on the other hand, the rule dictates that they must respond petition rights of general interest must be answered in the first 15 working days, according to Law 1755 of 2015 in accordance with Article 23 of the Constitution which reads "has the right to submit respectful requests to the authorities on grounds of general or private interest and to obtain a prompt resolution". As a result, it is evident that in practice this does not happen, and other mechanisms such as tutela must be resorted to in order to guarantee the constitutional right in , increasing the workload of the courts, For example, authorising surgery for a patient who suffers from morbid obesity and needs to be operated on, but as this is not authorised in his medical plan, it must be a judge who authorises it in connection with the right to life. All of this means that by not solving simple procedures with artificial intelligence, we wear out the system by filing the same application in many entities, standing in line, asking for permission at work so that you can do the procedure, spending money on transport, exposing yourself to crime, an accident, among other things. We do not measure the great importance of creating a tool that works throughout the national territory, with this we can avoid and streamline the system that is currently stagnant, about 7.4 hours [1] it takes a citizen to fulfill its management, also at the end of those hours the person may attend the place that does not correspond, for that reason should go to the right place to spend more time, therefore a tool with the help of artificial intelligence, It is a notorious fact that the more time, the more population, and that is one of the drawbacks that there is not so much human capacity in the entities to provide information or support to citizens, so it is necessary to seek technological support to sectorize problems, solving in a timely manner the attention to the citizen, in the same way the idea is to multiply the number of citizens in the same way. mimic human responsiveness in public administration with the aim of making the IA superior in terms of speed, accuracy and efficiency, which will provide statistics to show how many procedures can be completed successfully per day, month and year.

- Specific objective

Develop technological tools with an emphasis on AI that support the quality of service to citizens in the area of the Mobility Secretariat to significantly improve citizen service, for this situation it is necessary to develop specific technological tools. The following is a presentation of possible technological tools that can improve the provision of administrative services to the inhabitants of the Colombian territory:

-Conversational bot: This is software that uses artificial intelligence to interact with stakeholders. At the same time, this tool can provide replicas of answers that have the same factual relationship, being this fast and accurate to the usual questions of the people, with the plus of solving their inconvenience, not only that it is a shallow conversation, where the citizen is before with more doubts, the question must be related to the subject that handles the entity and over time be polishing the quality of the answers, The (AI) stores data, classifies them and in turn can generate statistics to measure the acceptance of the solution to the problems that afflicted the interested parties, without the need to go to a public sector entity, allowing to shorten waiting times, with this we can adapt a message according to their needs. Likewise, bots can be arranged to perform tasks, such as processing a request and processing it.

-Recognising data: Artificial intelligence has the capacity to manage large amounts of data, and thus locate the best response from the citizen in support of the procedure to be dealt with and identify schemes and guidelines in all areas of public administration.

-Connection of artificial intelligence (metaverse) of each entity in a cloud that is part of the public administration to have a compendium of frequent answers and greater ease of finding specific information for each case, it is necessary to be in accordance with Law 1581 of 2012 on data protection, since in some cases it will need information that only the interested party knows, manage procedures such as an authorisation for a surgery to a patient, to make a loan without the need to go to a bank in person, a procedure before the Dian (Directorate of Taxes and National

Customs), to express a complaint to a public service provider, answers in terms of petition rights to avoid saturating the judicial jurisdiction with tutelas, among thousands of issues that may arise in the administration as each area has special issues, the above to achieve a fast and unmediated attention to the citizen.

On the other hand, implementing AI to analyse large amounts of information that fits the particular need, improving the citizen's experience, to start with, the citizen's need must be parameterised and a solution must be available that allows them to be satisfied with the procedure, this can be anything from finding the best transport to get to a place, to providing administrative acts, products or services.

Then establish the automation of repetitive tasks with AI, which allows to improve the problems that afflict citizens with the public sector, this technique encompasses the use of parameters, formulas, patterns and machine learning concepts leading to decision making based on the information collected, without the need for the human being to be aware of the tasks resolved, generating a measurable database, where it is possible to keep track of how many procedures were answered in a given time, and to adjust parameters in order to gradually change the outlook for citizens in terms of public service provision.

2. THEORETICAL FRAMEWORK AND DEVELOPMENT

First all, this section will be studied with the support of Juan Ignacio Criado who, considering his path, is an example of authority to follow and for this reason it is worth mentioning in this final degree work. The author's domain topics are especially those related to the impact of information technology and communication and digital social networks in the public sector, he won a Julian Marias award in 2106 by the community of Madrid for the best researcher under 40 years old, in turn he was the first Spanish to be a researcher at Oxford internet institute in 2007, one of the works that stand out is the following "Las Administraciones Públicas En La Era Del Gobierno Abierto. Gobernanza Inteligente Para Un Cambio De Paradigma En La Gestión Pública", which will be studied, given the scope that represents opportunities derived from the new wave of technological innovation in the public sector.In this sense, Criado considers that public management is undergoing recent changes with the support of new social technologies, which permeate public organisations, known as intelligent governance, which seeks to situate the administered in the face of the variables that may arise and collaborations between employees and public organisations, and aims to provide an approach to the reality the management of technologies in contemporary public administrations. In a context in which social technologies have made their way into our societies, as in all economic, cultural or political contexts, the Artificial intelligence is playing an important role as a tool that we can implement in our daily life where it specifies the daily tasks to the public administration, solving the procedures of the citizens. These changes demand that the dialogue between the public administration and the administered is a transition; the State must provide the means for technology to be in every corner of the country so that it does not fall into a social gap where few can enjoy technological access and are still stuck wasting time carrying out procedures that should be of immediate response.

This fact has led to a lack of taste between the state and the public, since on the one hand, citizens do not have the appropriate technology and the government does not have as a priority to address issues of vital importance such as simplifying procedures with the support of artificial intelligence tools. This is when the author tries to envision the processes of open and collaborative public innovation to solve collective problems together with the citizens, in this case with the creation of specialised software for each issue that afflicts the citizens, in his words, that the administration be open and collaborative, in the same way, implementing the opening of public data, new social technologies and intelligent listening to what happens in the environment, accessing public administration to think of new methodologies to process the work processes and the relationship with the citizens.

For this reason, it is novel in terms of its relevance in the field. This is because it marks a point of view ignored until its arrival, in the sense that it shows a reading of power relations where the citizen does not have a south or a north, and does not organise to advance in the procedures, but complains daily in public transport, social networks and among friends, according to The author believes that technology, citizens and public administration must work in harmony, involving intelligent governance in the work of the State, in order to get out of backwardness, applying a change in the dynamics of simplification of procedures, bringing the administered closer to the administration.

In other words, the way Criado sees public value is that the projects are able to solve the precise public problems of a specific political community, and this seems to challenge what we are used to seeing, so it is important to change the chip and give entry to this type of technological support that will facilitate our daily lives. Thus, the end of this section is approaching, but not before developing the concept that Carles Ramió. (2019) provides with respect to the traditional processes are permeated by clientelism and corruption, for this reason it is a great opportunity to implement a new conceptual model that helps to improve transparency, with the help of a proactive strategy, taking advantage of the technological era to modernise the technical capacity of public administrations and to resolve many of their difficulties, not only conceptual, but organisational, in order to provide a better public service.

2.1 The mirror of the District Secretary of Mobility

Regarding the creation of different public sector entities, Bogotá's council passed agreement 257 in 2006, founding the District Mobility Secretariat, specifically in article 105, which reads: "The District Mobility Secretariat is hereby created. The District Secretariat of Mobility will start operating when the Mayor adopts its internal organisation and staffing plan and once they have been approved by the Mayor's Office. The corresponding public servants were incorporated"[2], starting work on 2 January of the following year with a mission focused on planning, management, and development in aspects of transit and transport.

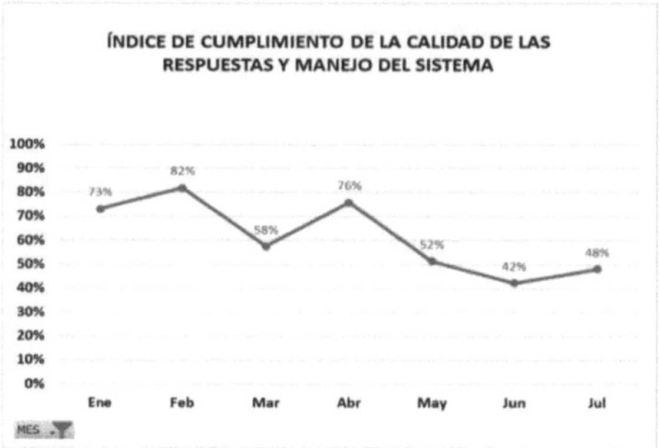

Fuente: Evaluación mensual de calidad y oportunidad

The above graph demonstrates the poor quality of user care, where the only thing that is provided is 48% of the total number of petitions filed are answered, and this is due to the low number of petitions received. trained personnel to carry out the work, in addition to the rotation of workers because the vast majority are service providers with contracts lasting 3 to 6 months and when renewing the workforce they must be trained for about a month so that they can take the normal rhythm of production, as they must handle many applications, including Sicon (Intranet, where proceedings are uploaded and internal procedures are consulted, such as knowing the status of a vehicle and the number of fines), Runt (consultative to take screenshots and know vehicle information), Orfeo (platform where PQRSD arrive and are answered), at the same time the workload is exhaustive because they assign overdue or expired rights of petition to the people who are arriving to the office, I noticed in the work area my colleagues working from 7:00 a.m. to 7:00 p.m. and they had to work from 7:00 a.m. to 7:00 p.m. and they were not able to answer the requests, which is impossible:00 am to 7:00 pm and weekends achieve the objectives, even so as there were few assistants the goals of the entity were not met, then I show two graphs of requests where 11381 expired requests are evidenced to July this year which is increasing, in December the number increases because people consume alcoholic beverages, there are more warnings, people become intolerant by eagerness to purchase, views, travel among others. On the other hand, these unanswered petitions are going to congest the judicial apparatus with tutelas for violating the right to receive clear, precise and congruent answers[4] from the administration, generating a chain of congestion and reprocesses in the public administration.

Fuente: Sistema Distrital para la Gestión de Peticiones Ciudadanas – Bogotá te escucha

The same happens with the proceedings that are presented in the challenge of comparendos, since as a general rule for a citizen to make a removal of a vehicle, which is called exit of yards, for having committed an infraction that warrants immobilisation of the vehicle, according to the National Land Traffic Code Law 769 of 2002); it takes approximately 3, 4 hours or more depending on the complexity of the procedure, also the number of people who go to the service centre for different procedures, such as: -challenge of comparendos, exit of yards, request for caducidades and/or prescriptions, In many cases, I often observed people who went several days to carry out the procedure because they did not receive an answer or a solution to the problem, the traffic authorities have different positions and do not have clear guidelines on certain issues such as the scrapping of a vehicle, some give the authorisation to remove the vehicle with commitments, and others indicate that it must be renewed for a newer one, ordering dismantling, issues that with the help of the AI can be resolved by adjusting edges that direct the same positions for similar cases.

As can be seen in the images above, it is unheard of how long citizens have to wait to carry out a procedure, not to mention the journeys and permits they have to ask for to attend these procedures, in this case the appointment scheduling system failed, causing chaos outside the secretary's office, but it is not only on that day that this number of people is seen, this is the general rule of the The difference is that they have created a space for them to be followed, so that the mob is not seen outside but inside the organisation. According to the District Services Directorate where the study and the graphs were carried out, the following observation was determined:"According to the findings, the requirements do not comply with the criterion of timeliness, since the responses were issued outside the terms established in the regulations in force. The requirements do not comply with management of the system, since the publication of the responses in the application was extemporaneous. The entity must upload the responses to the system within the days established by law to respond to the request, as established in numeral 5.2 Generalities of the registration of Petitions of the Manual for the Management of Citizen Petitions"(8). , it is necessary to change this methodology of attention to citizens and the procedures they develop, first of all, I wanted to implement the use of virtual technology (metaverse) with the help of AI in the District Mobility Secretariat. In the first place, the objectives are aimed at improving user service satisfaction, and secondly, in addition, the scams promoted by the so-called "jaladores" who are outside the entity hunting for the unwary, who generally swindle people with charges ranging from50.000 and $150.000 pesos, in the case of photo comparendos, and can reach up to $10.000.000 million pesos in the case of a grade III drunkenness offence, as the maximum penalty for failing to allow the to take the test on the road or to take the test in the street is $50.000 and $150.000 pesos, respectively. refusal to do so carries a fine of approximately $46,000,000 million pesos, which in dollars is approximately $9517.42.

In short, for a Colombian citizen to be able to pay this type of sanction, he/she must save one legal minimum wage for 46 months. However, the main objective of the second issue is to put an end to fraudsters outside the Secretariat of Mobility, this is a problem that the Secretariat has been dealing with since it was founded, they have tried to implement strategies with police accompaniment or surveillance of officials but these have been threatened and for security reasons they decided to continue with them around the facilities, In any case, the solution would allow for greater revenue collection for the entity, since the citizen would have access to educational courses to obtain benefits such as 50% reduction of the fine, if the petitioner during the 5 days following the imposition of the comparendo attends the course, which consists of a two-hour training course to ensure that he/she does not violate the traffic code. At present, in order to access this benefit, the citizen must attend the course, which generates congestion in the entity and this is where outsiders take advantage of the opportunity to persuade the person in question by promising to eliminate fines or sanctions for sums of money, claiming that they have acquaintances within the state body.

In any case, the "jaladores" would have no room to continue obtaining income from citizens because the vast majority of transactions would be carried out from home.

Currently, the Bogota Mobility Secretariat is one of the entities that has the highest revenue collection, according to the number of vehicles in transit and in breach of the national traffic code, but the good treatment is not observed because there is an overload of work with employees and the number of staff is not sufficient. versus the number of angry citizens who arrive in search of a prompt solution to their vehicle's situation. That said, it is necessary to change the scenario and move it to the virtual field, saving travel time of citizens, management that can be executed from home or , in turn people can not be swindled with false information provided by the "pullers". The mechanisms used to respond to the requests are then carried out through correspondence platforms, where each request has a number and a deadline to respond to the process, this is how it currently works in the Secretariat of Mobility, the drawback is that the requests are massive and the people responsible for assigning the requests within the entity do not do well, I make this statement because in the vast majority of requests should be reassigned to the corresponding groups often a request went through up to three different areas exceeding the terms of response. The solution to this problem is to virtualise with the help of artificial intelligence, so that the requests are grouped together and sent to the corresponding area, and to collect more information when the request is filed so as not to generate misunderstandings and so that it can be easily transferred to the area in charge of the matter, and also to automate the responses to the rights of petition to similar questions to help decongest where the official can show personal data such as name, ID card, vehicle licence plate and comparendo to approve the sending of the response. In this case, the aim is to get to know and listen to the people administered, as they are extremely important for there to be a communicative exchange for the benefit of citizen attention, attending to the responses with guidelines of satisfaction, perception and quality. Consequently, a virtual forum can be used every quarter in the entities, where the community can contribute and discuss ideas to generate citizen satisfaction in the creation of regulations or activities to be carried out in favour of the administration. Similarly, the stage of the budget cycle can be classified within the Secretariat of Mobility in order to diagnose the start and termination of contractors at the beginning of the year, because contracts are made for 3 or 6 months, and while an addition or new contract is made, in the following year, This affects the provision of services to the public, and saturates the workload of those who are added to the contract, taking into account the fact that the community is delayed in order to be able to process a vehicle in December and January (contract termination dates), which increases the waiting time by 45%, It is therefore important to introduce a budget project where artificial intelligence is promoted, so that the entity always has software developers who are aware of the algorithms and do not have these gaps of time and uncertainty, where those affected are the officials due to the increased workload and the citizens who must wait twice the established time to carry out their procedure.

In short, the concept of public servant and/or public official, introduced in the 1991 Constitution, includes all persons who are at the service of the State and the community, to recall, with this expression, that the exercise of public power has as its raison d'être the achievement of the ends of society and the State and not personal benefit. In other words, a public servant is any person who is in the service of the State and exercises "public function" in its various forms[9]. These behaviours are determined by the knowledge, skills, abilities, values, attitudes and aptitudes that the public servant must possess and demonstrate in the exercise of his or her work.Change managers inspect the implementation of what can be advanced in an organisation. They are in charge of ensuring that the new technological strategy is carried out and fully complied with, as they have the power to generate changes in an organisation. In the specific case of the Secretary of Mobility, Deyanira Ávila Moreno is a cadastral engineer and geodesist with a degree from the Universidad Distrital Francisco José de Caldas; with a postgraduate degree in Urban Environmental Management from the Universidad Piloto de Colombia; she is also a WRI Road Safety auditor and an internal auditor in Quality Management Systems ISO 9001:2015, with a career of 10 years in the transit and transport sector occupying positions as director of Mobility Planning, office advisor and deputy director of the bicycle and pedestrian.

Of which she has dedicated more than 10 years to the Mobility Sector, she was Director of Mobility Planning, Office Advisor and first Deputy Director of Bicycle and Pedestrian in the Secretariat of Mobility,[10] in the year 2019 Bogotá occupied the post of 12th in the copenhagenize index of the world top 20, being the capital city with the best qualification. Bogotá was also recognised at the 5th Guangzhou Award, a competition for innovation in urban planning, as one of the 30 outstanding cities, carrying out temporary cycle routes in 2021.

Likewise, this directive with its background and experience is likely to articulate what will be developed in this final master's thesis, where an AI tool will be implemented in the mobility secretariat so that it can later be expanded to all state entities, to the point that the public does not have to waste time in taking transport, queuing up and exposing themselves to risks in the street, as we can see according to the Ombudsman's Office, "through 19 official reports of consummation and Early Warnings 010-21 and 005-22, the city at permanent risk, different criminal gangs are disputing the control of territories and illegal economies"[11] in different localities of Bogotá. Therefore, by making the process virtual, we prevent the actions of these criminal gangs in the formalities sector, thus decongesting the roads of the capital and improving the movement of citizens by not using public transport or private services, which is one of the great advantages of starting this type of project. mobility, as the panorama can be encompassed at city level, generating legitimacy and peace of mind on the part of citizens.

In summary, the mobility secretary can be an agent of change playing a significant role, as it can move from one extreme to another the core behaviour of the entity, encouraging people to have positive thoughts on a specific topic, offer different ways of thinking to act in a given context following parameters for the organisation, which in this case is to systematise the reception of PQRSD, internal distribution, equal responses to similar cases such as the citizen requesting prescription or expiration of a comparendo, In turnno challenges or yard exits are made in person and everything is done electronically where the algorithms are manipulated so that when the person files a challenge a folder is created in the cloud where the administrative sanctioning process is carried out, such as the opening of the process, evidence, allegations and finally the ruling, which the employees of the secretariat can save the steps mentioned and dedicate themselves to making the rulings only, these can be notified electronically with the prior authorisation of the parties.

The White Paper[12] on artificial intelligence identified several aspects and one of them is that it has a high impact on our society, as it covers a chain of actions that serves to facilitate the tasks of an entire community, in turn has application in the public sector, especially in the means of transport, among others, highlighting a reduction in operating costs. However, it is important that this creates confidence, since we are talking about something new, which people are not used to living with, and they must be reassured; it is also important to have a regulation that frames the parameters and limits of artificial intelligence applied to citizen care, respecting the fundamental rights of each individual. Another aspect is that citizens fear that they have no defence when it comes to safeguarding their rights and security in the face of the imbalances that may result from the algorithms that the applications may present; while it is true that artificial intelligence can be used to provide security to society and ensure that their fundamental rights are not violated, it is nevertheless important to regulate the procedures by constantly adjusting the parameters, making progress in systematic improvement to provide peace of mind to citizens. It is convenient to use software to measure performance within the Mobility Secretariat in order to be precise and objective, since the human factor can alter the results, and in a country like Colombia, the outcome can vary due to the fact of being a friend, a recommendation, or due to criteria external to the work environment, in order to generate calls for attention for past issues that have happened between the evaluator and the evaluated. Therefore, a software would deliver clean, ordered information, generating a history in the time, without prejudices of the human being, managing to identify, the weaknesses of the employees, and like being able to improve the productivity of this one; bearing in mind that every person is different this type of programs seem to me suitable to be able to stand out the weaknesses of the worker. In addition to having this type of programme, it is possible to personalise the information collected, generate statistics and measure the trajectory of a worker immediately, as opposed to the manual system which is not precise, even though the personnel in charge of human talent may be incapacitated, they may also leave the The key to the drawer where the performance evaluations are kept at home, a thousand other excuses for not having the information in real time, making it difficult to make decisions at times when the entity needs it.

2.1.1 History and evolution of AI

Within the literature on the history and evolution of the subject in question, Luis Eduardo Munera, doctor of the Polytechnic University of Madrid, affirms that since we were homo sapiens, artificial intelligence began with intellectual faculties, and later we can see the first narration written in the book the Iliada in the year 750 B.C. approximately.C approximately, where it was narrated "the scene of Achilles' mother in the workshop or forge of Efestos, which is in a laboratory of that time, full of automatisms and it is told that the God who had deformed feet, in order to walk was helped by two female robots of solid gold and who had intelligence"(13). In the mid-19th century, mathematician Ada Lovelace created the first algorithm intended to be implemented in a machine, laying the foundations of computation. Ada envisaged that the creation "could act on things other than numbers... the engine (the machine) could compose elaborate and scientific musical pieces of any degree of complexity or length".[14] Years later, Ada's view became a reality thanks to Artificial Intelligence (AI).The foundational moment of "artificial intelligence", on other hand, was developed in a field of study, in 1956 is a conference in Darmouth, USA. United States, which was organised by John McCarthy, Marvin Minsky, among others, so-called pioneers of AI. Four of the attendees were awarded the Turing Prize (Nobel Prize in computer science) for their tributes to artificial intelligence. A common idea among the attendees is that thinking is a form of computation that is not unique to humans. Thus, it is hypothesised that human intelligence is possible to simulate in machines. It is appropriate to say that over time artificial intelligence should be regularised and coupled to society so that it facilitates our daily tasks, which in this case should focus on citizen services in public administration. Initially, in every era, imagining that technology was more than just things could be a mere fiction; today the idea is that they are more than tools that can help us in our daily lives.Positively, the selfish thinking of our state is what holds back a civilisation that deals with human beings, but what about immaterial entities that have legal personality? Mobility secretariats, local councils, administrative bodies or the state itself are an example of how modernity demands that they be made an autonomous part of processes that require them to exercise their duties and rights with the help of new technologies. In the case of AI, these precepts are united in : the duty and right to exist and to be preserved. A duty to exist that is exercised natively as a scenario of harmony between human beings and technological changes, and a right that translates into the benefit of coexisting without further mediation.Now, it is necessary to open specialised scenarios that determine the assistance to the population, we see that at present we need to improve the provision of service to the city dwellers and the best option is with the help of technology that classifies The time it takes each person approximately 7.4 hours to carry out a procedure, as I will explain below. In short, it is a question of support and coexistence. In the same way that people have granted themselves rights, in the same way technology deserves it for the mere fact of existing and being a form that accompanies us in life, only that it must be regulated. Dogmatically this sounds wonderful, but in practice it is more complex than it seems. It is here that the question arises, how to use machines in the public sector, for the benefit of citizens? The position is that the state has not given it the real importance and the resources it requires. There are already natural and legal persons, now it is time to name artificial intelligence as a subject, as it has developed throughout history. However, it is clear that it alone approach a state and demand that they implement it. It is a matter of commitment to the country to scale up, becoming more competitive, at least by lowering the waiting rate in the daily procedures of citizens, a figure issued by the Inter-American Development Bank. Having become a little clearer about how the information is integrated, the area of application will be shown, recognising legal personality by analysing reality. This will be done by examining cases, concepts and reasons that led to decisions - apparently aiming at the use of means to help solve everyday problems in public administration.

2.1.2 Areas of application at IA

This chapter will be aimed at showing the different AI systems and which one serves to address the problem. Natural languages: focuses on language translation, which allows for the use of a with an operating system and be user-friendly. Expert systems: In this field the information is based on qualified personnel and is as close to reality as possible. Robotics: Robot movements, e.g. a robotic hand or a robot hand, are assemblies.

Perceptual problems: Recognition of patterns in objects and voice commands or defects in parts. Learning: Modelling of behaviours for its subsequent implementation on computers.[15]In this way, the system that benefits us is the expert because its program will be directed by qualified personnel and will indicate to the software the different paths that the citizen has in each state agency, and thus program the assembly of possibilities, through artificial intelligence classifying the task effectively, an example of application can be put into practice in the Secretariat of Mobility, per in the capital, Bogotá 28.964 comparendos[16] are made, for infringing the rules of The Supercade on Calle 13 (where courses are held to obtain discounts on fines if they are presented within the first 5 days after the fine has been imposed, or if the person wishes to contest the fines because they disagree with them, as well as the process of removing a vehicle from the yard, when a car is immobilised for endangering road users) can be decongested. In this place there are more than 500 people a day, queuing endlessly to be able to carry out any of the above-mentioned procedures, as it is a manual job, it is wasteful because it must be attended to one by one and the staff who collaborate is not enough for so many people. On the contrary, if AI is used, it could be automated by comparendo, so that they can access the courses, quickly, and issue administrative acts that give permission to remove the vehicle easily with security questions that only the owner knows, to avoid loss vehicles, After this we move on to the challenge of comparendos, which can be done virtually but that the hearing is conducted by bots, to decongest the sector, as it must ensure due process and provide evidence by the person concerned. In addition to helping with the provision of public administration service to citizens, it would also help to decongest part of the city because all people must go in person to carry out a procedure, and if this is implemented in all sectors we can see a decrease in traffic jams improving the flow of vehicles, as our city is the fourth worst in vehicular traffic[17] , not to mention the constant dangers that we citizens face.

Figura 3.2 ANALOGÍA ENTRE EL EXPERTO HUMANO Y EL SISTEMA EXPERTO.

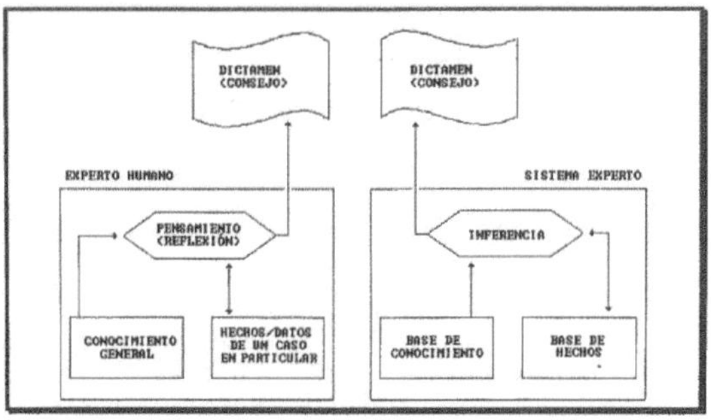

This computer system functionally incorporates the knowledge of an experienced human, enabling it to answer, explain and justify its answers. This, like all definitions, gives us an idea. Basically, what you get in an expert system is combination of human knowledge. More precisely, to solve problems at intelligently,all we need to do is mimic the way people solve problems, applying it in software that will provide a solution to the facts presented. Thus, an expert system can solve a problem in particular area of knowledge in the same way that a professional in a particular field would solve it. The first systems created were essentially diagnostic systems in medicine, capable of determining how a medical professional would do it. If you wonder why you came to this conclusion, it should argue and explain the answer. "The areas of application of expert systems are grouped by types of problems, which are basically: interpretation, prediction, diagnosis, planning and control"(19). This is what is necessary to be able to deal with the problems that are currently arising in all the entities of the Colombian State for the system that helps decision-making. Next, I show a comparative table of AI and natural intelligence.

Cuadro 1.1 COMPARACIÓN INTELIGENCIA ARTIFICIAL-INTELIGENCIA NATURAL.

INTELIGENCIA ARTIFICIAL	INTELIGENCIA NATURAL
RASGOS COMUNES	
*Se acrecienta con la experiencia *Obsolescencia y empobrecimiento por falta de uso	*Se acrecienta con la experiencia *Obsolescencia y empobrecimiento por falta de uso
ASPECTOS POSITIVOS	**ASPECTOS NEGATIVOS**
*Suele estar bien documentada. Se puede reproducir y transmitir con facilidad *Posibilidad de acumular conocimiento permanentemente *Es consistente *Perdura tras la desaparición de la persona *Coste razonable	*Documentación escasa *No resulta fácil su transmisión *Es efímera y no permanente *Es irregular *Desaparece con la persona *Coste alto
ASPECTOS NEGATIVOS	**ASPECTOS POSITIVOS**
*De forma general no es creativa *No forma parte de la cultura general de una persona	*Es creativa *Forma parte de la cultura general de una persona

2.1.3 Recognise the legal personality of the IA

To begin with, the legal nature of artificial intelligence systems has been a hotly debated topic. To examine the legal issue, our laws, especially in the Colombian civil code in articles 73,74 and 633 distinguish between a natural person and a legal person. Personal characteristics include: age, sex, originating from a human being or condition. On the other hand, the characteristics of juridical persons are: fictitious persons of two types, corporations or companies and public charitable foundations. Legal personality implies that these entities are capable of exercising rights. and to enter into obligations, as well as to be represented in a judicial and extra-judicial setting. Is it feasible for an AI mechanism applied to public administration to be endowed with the above-mentioned attributes? AI procedures have, as a rule, the ability to interact; a reading of the outside; and they are endowed with a degree of independence that is in turn spontaneous. In addition, is it possible to grant legal recognition to artificial intelligence systems for having the above characteristics? To answer this question, we must consider whether the software that is implemented to help citizens in automatic procedures can exercise rights and incur obligations, I think not, they are only tools that would have an intellectual property protection, to create this mechanism to assist in the provision of public service. An example of this is acquiring a Windows licence for the computers of an entity, where an annual membership fee must be paid for it to continue working and making the necessary updates. This can be transferred to the administration with systematised procedures that guide, help and solve the problems of the citizens, organising the information in a precise way, either from a technological application or directly in the institution. The issue of granting a legal personality is for the future and in the face of other issues such as robots that resemble humans and can cause positive and negative things, and they want to categorise them under the name of electronic personality in order to establish civil liability for the damage that can be caused by the use of these elements. For greater understanding, NIEVA FENOLL[21] emphatically considers that there can be no question of the creation of an electronic personality in terms of attribution of liability. It is difficult to hold a robot liable, given that it is not a sentient being. Liability therefore lies with the creator or programmer of the robot. A current example of the recognition of rights of this kind for the most advanced robots and AI systems can be found in Saudi Arabia where "Sophia" [(22)], which has been interviewed in different parts of the world, was granted honorary citizenship as a humanoid with an artificial intelligence engine.In summary, the recognition of the legal personality of AIs is a matter of discussion and could develop in the future, currently most regulatory systems do not grant legal personality to AIs.

2.1.4 Jurisprudential guidance on IA

This year a judge in Cartagena made a ruling with the help of ChatGPT in favour of an autistic child, the conclusion of the order was the exemption of payments for transfers, and procedures that had to be done to the child, because the mother did not have the necessary resources to pay for the treatments. From that moment on, a debate about the use of

AI in the courts germinated, with little acceptance from the sector because the platform that was used is something that does not is regulated, and certain and arguable rights are being debated, even more so with regard to a minor.

In times of pandemic, thanks to decree 806 of 2020 and subsequent law 2213 of 2022, measures were adopted to implement new technologies in judicial proceedings, with the aim of activating the processes and adapting the attention to users of the justice service, but this was limited to holding virtual hearings and having the technological mechanisms to preside over the proceedings.

In criminal law, artificial intelligence can be used to analyse large databases and assist as a tool for judges to make decisions, but not to rely on them. AI systems can examine sources of law, jurisprudence, recent case law, testimony, evidence used, doctrine, reports, etc. to assist judges in assessing the responsibility of a defendant.

In addition, for the topic at hand, we will bring the definition provided by the European Commission:

"The term artificial intelligence (AI) is applied to systems that manifest intelligent behaviour, as they are able to analyse their environment and take action - with a certain degree of autonomy - in order to achieve specific goals·

Thus, as artificial intelligence has been used in the justice system, tools can be developed to improve citizen service, in any entity that can classify information in a matter of seconds, on subjects that a This can take several minutes, and there are not enough staff for so many services, which can be solved by using applications or computers in the public sector.

2.2 Algorithms and models used on IA

According to the Rae, the algorithm is an ordered and finite set of operations that makes it possible to find the solution to a problem"(24).

We use artificial intelligence every day and often don't realise it. For example, when we ask a technology platform to set an alarm for the next day to attend a meeting or when we unlock a mobile phone with the help of facial recognition. Algorithms provide livelihoods for these interesting tools. In short, algorithms are level-by-level instructions that help a computer perform calculations. In this way, artificial intelligence uses notation to create devices that learn from experience, adapt to new situations and perform tasks as any of us would. The use of algorithms in administrative activity falls entirely within the framework of legitimacy. Thus, with regard to administrative procedures of a "massive" or serial nature, the consideration of resorting to an automated decision, in order to contribute to speeding up procedures and guaranteeing their accuracy and the predictability of the results, has long been accepted (Vaccari, 2019). Italian jurisprudence has accepted the option of appealing to mechanical solutions of decision in case of of instructions repetitive without margin of discretion, and in fact was sometimes in favour of resorting to solutions that were "automated". [25] One of the advantages systems and algorithms applied to public administration is that they are unlikely to be permeated by corruption and are impartial, especially in the conduct of back-to-back operations, which would help Transparency International's Corruption Perceptions Index 2020[26], as Colombia scored 39 out of 100, ranking 92nd out of 180 countries evaluated. Even when by virtue of the law certain categories of intellectual property rights must be recognised to legal persons, we speak of derivative or secondary ownership of rights,14 but the original ownership always corresponds to a natural or physical person: "the author". And an author is the person who conceives and produces a literary work or creates and performs an artistic work. So, effectively, if the AI algorithm is considered to be an "object" and not a subject of , under current law it cannot be attributed the status of author.

These projects are a new way of expressing human creativity, as has been said, there is now a tendency to humanise the capabilities of the machine; it produces because it was designed to be able to do what it is ordered to do. In short, there is always a human in some of the tasks that are done so that the algorithm achieves the desired result. Thus, it is in line with Ríos Ruiz (2001), who almost two decades ago warned that the products of AI (which can qualify as works) should not enter the public domain, because in them it is possible to determine one or more eventual holders, who will be the people who make the adjustments necessary for the creation of the work and the final result produced by the device.[27]

2.2.1 Analysing the reality

In agreement with BENITEZ, Raúl the objective of the AI is "to emulate some of the human intellectual faculties in artificial systems"[28], and it is the project that we look for to emulate the workforce of the entities improving the benefit of the service, shortening the time of wait of the citizens that is around 7,4 hours[29], by tramite with help of a technological tool based on AI would encasillaría the subject to treat of the citadino, giving him response of immediate form, even without leaving home, saving money to move, the time mentioned, also helping in security issues because the person would not be available to the offender or to the processor who is outside the entities charging sums of money for sneaking into the attention line or indicating that it advances the procedures, thanks to a friend who is an official, then I show a table of the hours that a person spends performing a procedure by country.

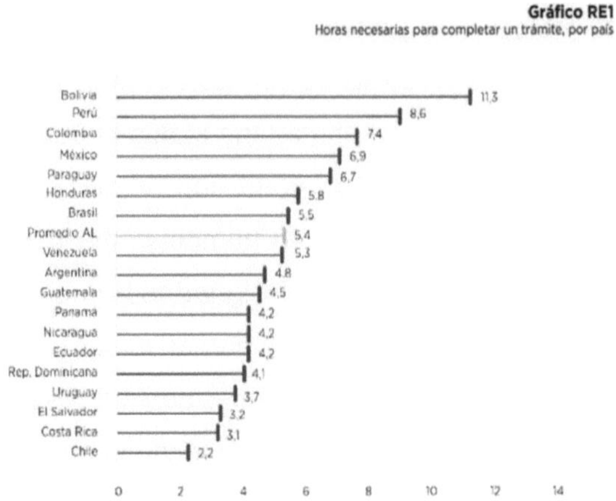

Basically, artificial intelligence (AI) in Colombia has experienced exponential growth in the last decade. In terms of research, Colombia has several research centres that are dedicated to the advancement of artificial intelligence. They are advanced by pioneering universities in the field, such as the Universidad de los Andes, Universidad de Antioquia and, among others. Similarly, the application of AI in the industrial sector has seen advances in areas such as health and agriculture. For example, in the health sector, AI-assisted diagnostic systems have been developed help doctors detect diseases early.

In this sense, businesses are beginning to implement AI-based solutions to improve the operation of their products, the manipulation of databases and the customer service experience. It is also being used in the financial sector, which has led to the discovery of fraud and the development of financial services more in line with the needs of each citizen. For these reasons, there are challenges with AI in Colombia, as in most countries. These challenges contain two concerns, one about the privacy of stored and classified data, and the other about algorithmic bias, which must be addressed by raising awareness of the help that technology can provide in the public sector. In the first case, the software must be configured so that classified information does not leak out and, in turn, it must have computer security so that it cannot be hacked; in the second case, with the facts and the change of procedures that will be carried out quickly, confidence in the algorithms used by humans will be generated.

In short, AI in Colombia has resolved to invest in competitions to manage research progress. It is likely that AI will rescue an increasingly important role in our land, initially driving innovation in all fields where automation exists.

2.2.1.1 AI and the ethical

The European Parliament set up a committee on AI with the aim of analysing the impact it is having and setting out a way forward. Taking into The commission presented a final report on 3 May 2022, which took one year and six months to complete. To this end, it recommends a series of measures in the following areas:

- Promoting investment, innovation and European leadership in AI, supporting key sectors such as health, education, transport or environment. It is also proposed to create a European data space and digital infrastructures to access and exchange of data and information between Member States and public and private actors.
- The guarantee and respect for fundamental rights, democratic values and the rule of law in the development and use of AI. To this end, it seeks to establish a harmonised legal framework based on ethical principles, such as transparency, accountability and non-discrimination. It also calls for the strengthening of procedural safeguards and control and oversight mechanisms to prevent possible abuses or harm caused by AI-based systems or devices.
- Protect consumers, workers and citizens from risks or negative

consequences arising from the misuse or malicious use of AI. It calls for ensuring a high level of safety and quality in AI-based products and services; promoting digital skills and lifelong learning; ensuring decent working conditions; preserving privacy and protection of personal data; among other measures.

- The promotion of effective international cooperation with other countries or international organisations to define global standards on AI that are consistent with European values [31].

In 1987, M. Mitchell Waldrop published an article in The AI Magazine titled

"A Question of Responsibility'. In it, he outlines the concept of "machine ethics" and proposes the need to control the values, assumptions and purposes introduced by programmers in order to realise that decision-making capacity. [32]

In particular, three ethical problems may arise:

"1) The manufacture of robots and the programming of artificial intelligence systems, where respect for the dignity, privacy and security of persons must be guaranteed.

2) The performance of functions by robots and artificial intelligence systems involving ethical decision-making and autonomous and unpredictable actions, with the possible consideration of these as moral agents and the possible problem of determining liability for damage generated by such systems.

3) The treatment that legal systems should give to artificial intelligence systems and their possible consideration as moral patients or directly as subjects of law"(33).

The human being perceives AI systems as a range of knowledge, but with mistrust that the machine will fall into error and not fully comply with the complexity of the matter, on the contrary, as I explained above, the algorithm must be programmed over time, making updates for improvement to avoid this type of leakage and discontent that can be generated in civil society.

2.2.1.2 Principles of AI in the public sector

In Colombia, there is a compiled programme called COMPES 3975 of 2019, issued by the National Council for Economic and Social Policy, which talks about artificial intelligence and aims at the "strategic use of digital technologies in a broad manner, involving the public and private sectors with an emphasis on the use of ICTs as tools to boost productivity and promote the well-being of citizens, who are the beneficiaries and consumers of the goods and services that are produced. It also seeks to create the necessary conditions for the promotion of AI as one of the most important accelerators of this process without ignoring the potential of other digital technologies"[34]. Taking into account the broad field of application, it was unavoidable to establish 14 principles to guide AI in our territory:

1. AI market creation: this consists of mixing the sectors where designers, suppliers, intermediaries and consumers of this technology interact.
2. Prioritisation of market-creating innovations
3. Evidence-based policy and impact metrics for regulation.
4. Regulatory experimentation.
5. Easily accessible data infrastructure.
6. AI market as a generator of equity and inclusion.
7. Ethical framework AI and security.

8. Credible and consensual commitments.

9. Experimental environment for developing talent policies.

10. Universities and academic research as strategic actors in AI market creation.

11. Attracting international talent.

12. Developing evidence-based policies on the future of work.

13. The state as a facilitator and user of AI.

14. Continuous access to the knowledge of the international community.

Colombia is considered a successful country in the region in terms of mapping and implementing its National Strategy for Artificial Intelligence, although it is not enough to implement a project. However, in Colombia there have been significant efforts by the administration to digitally transmute the public sector, there are still great opportunities for improvement, and this is the beginning that projects new patterns for the implementation of AI. At the moment, the implementation of ICTs is not fulfilling its purpose of incorporating greater institutional strength, for reasons of corruption and socio-economic problems that abound in our country.Next, it is necessary to create the conditions for the creation of technological tools that can be implemented in the public sector, where the The beneficiaries are the administration and the administered overcoming outdated structures and ways of thinking everyday, where citizens are prepared to live in a comfort zone, even if they are bad, and we get used to the same because it is what we live from childhood, an example of this is that a minor accompanies his parent to perform any diligence, and one prepares oneself mentally that there are many hours to complete that duty, and so we grow up and normalise that it should take forever in public procedures, which a contrario sensu with the help of AI could be handled in minutes without leaving home, and spend that wasted time on productive things, obtaining greater social welfare.

3 CONCLUSIONS

The idea that public management should be autonomous with the help of AI is a task of hard work, both theoretical and practical, which must be protected as something natural and necessary for the survival of the media and the future population. The negligence of the public administration in allocating the necessary resources to support new technologies is a violation of society as a whole and is the gap that separates us from a first world country. For this reason, it is necessary to take advantage of legal mechanisms that effectively influence the construction of a healthy technical environment. In this case, enabling the door for AI to cover the District Mobility Secretariat, improving the provision of services to citizens. The above, being more relevant in the creation of specific algorithms for each sector and calling on the public to make the transition from traditional to new technological matters, as AI is the future and must be present in all territorial entities. Therefore, the idea is to convert mechanics into automation. It can be affirmed, then, that there is a predisposition towards a progressive technological vision, a product of a conscious responsibility in the appropriation of improving citizen care in order to advance at the pace that the passage of time brings us, and that this may be in favour of the proposed thesis. On the other hand, territorial analysis teaches that there are ways of reading languages and in this case it was seen how in the media one can see the non-conformism of the voices that try to capture the reality of waiting times longer than 7.4 hours (Inter-American Development Bank) and precisely, the way they do it is by describing situations that in the light of this era should not be happening. In conclusion, AI has great contributions to efficiency and productivity that can reform public administration and improve citizen service. On the other hand, new technologies can find solutions to different social problems, such as climate change, environmental degradation; when it is more systematised and people have full confidence in artificial intelligence, it is possible to open the spectrum towards the fight against crime, as long as freedoms, liberties and fundamental rights are respected as mentioned above. AI has been forged thanks to the role it plays in developed countries, whether implicit or not - and which is in force in the CONPES document and judicial decision as has been seen in this research work, in terms of jurisprudence AI has every field of application from medicine to programming an alarm clock with a voice command. For this reason, as mentioned above, the seed has already been planted in written form, but it must be adapted to the socio-economic reality that, for it to develop, the technological gaps that obscure regions far from the centre must be eliminated. In this way, it is important to reach all regions, but first implement an algorithm in a specific entity (District Secretariat of Mobility) that classifies the information and makes it easy to use in order to expand a specific formula for each entity, which translates into short processing times.

BIBLIOGRAPHICAL REFERENCES

Basic bibliography

-Criado, J. I. (2016). Public administrations in the era of open government. Smart governance for a paradigm shift in public management. Revista de Estudios Políticos, 173, 245-275. doi: http://dx.doi.org/10.18042/cepc/rep.173.07.

-RAMIÓ, Carles. Artificial intelligence and public administration: robots and humans sharing public service. Spanish Journal of Political Science. 2019, 207- 210.

Complementary bibliography

-BENJAMIN ROSETH ANGELA REYES CARLOS SANTISO. El fin del trámite eterno: Ciudadanos, burocracia y gobierno digital. Inter-American Development Bank [online]. June from 2018 [accessed on 1 of May 1 from 2023]. Available at: https://publications.iadb.org/es/el-fin-del-tramite-eterno-ciudadanos-burocracia-y- gobierno-digital

-Munera Salazar, L. E. (2000). Principles of Artificial Intelligence and Expert Systems. Cali, Colombia: Universidad Icesi. Available at: https://repository.icesi.edu.co/biblioteca_digital/handle/10906/4006

-Gutierrez, AAC (2018). History and evolution of the intelligence.artificial. https://revistasdex.uchile.cl/index.php/bits/issue/view/217

-Alfonso Galipienso, MI, Cazorla Quevedo, MA, Colomina Pardo, O., Escolano Ruiz, F., & Lozano Ortega, MA (2003). Inteligencia artificial: modelos, técnicas y áreas de aplicación. Ediciones Paraninfo.

-Fedemunicipios, P. (2022, 29 April). 90,741 traffic fines were imposed at the national level on month of April. Federation Colombian Federation de Municipios. https://www.fcm.org.co/90-741-comparendos-se-impusierona-nivel- national-in-the-month-of-april/

- AMADOR HIDALGO, Luis. Artificial intelligence and expert systems. University of Córdoba, Servicio de Publicaciones, 1996.

-Benitez, Raul et al. Inteligencia artificial avanzada. Barcelona: Editorial UOC, 2013.

-NIEVA FENOLL, J., Videoconference: "Inteligencia Artificial y Proceso Penal", Universitas Fundación, 22 July 2020. Online resource: https://www.youtube.com/watch?v=5BrCNVTPp0o.

-Open letter to the European Commission Artificial Intelligence and Robotics",Robotics Open Letter, available at http://www.robotics-openletter.eu/.

-EUROPEAN COMMISSION. Artificial Intelligence for Europe. COM (2018) 237 final, of 25.4. 218.DOUE{SWD (2018) 137 FINAL}. 2018, p.1.

-BBC World Technology (2017, 30 October). Sophia, the robot who has more rights than women in Saudi Arabia. https://www.bbc.com/mundo/noticias- 41803576.

-rae. (2023). algorithm. https://dle.rae.es/algoritmo.

-Carloni, Enrico. "AI, Algorithms and Public Administration in Italy. IDP. Journal of Internet, Law and Politics, 2020, no.30, https://doi.org/10.7238/idp.v0i30.3228

Label: index of perception. (2020). Label: index of perception.

https://transparenciacolombia.org.co/tag/indice-de-percepcion/

-Michelle Azuaje Pirela (2020). Legal protection of artificial intelligence products in the intellectual property system. Universidad Autónoma de Chile.

-European Parliament (2020). A European approach to excellence in AI. european parliament. https://digital-strategy.ec.europa.eu/es/policies/european-approach- artificial-intelligence

-JAVIER GONZALO GRANADO (2020). Roboethics and robot law. From the person to personality.

ACTION FOR RELIEF IN MATTERS RELATING TO THE RIGHT TO REQUEST-Appropriateness of

directly because it is a fundamental right of immediate application (n.d.). Gov.co. Retrieved 1 September 2023, from https://www.corteconstitucional.gov.co/relatoria/2018/t-206-18.htm

-Ministry of Information and Communications Technologies (2019, 8 November). NATIONAL COUNCIL OF ECONOMIC AND SOCIAL POLICY REPUBLIC OF COLOMBIA NATIONAL PLANNING DEPARTMENT. Document CONPES 3975.

Moreno, D. Á. (2022, 23 August). Deyanira Ávila Moreno, nueva Secretaria Distrital de Movilidad (Deyanira Ávila Moreno, new District Secretary of Mobility). Bogotá.gov.co; Deyanira Ávila Moreno, nueva Secretaria Distrital de Movilidad. https://bogota.gov.co/mi-ciudad/gabinete-distrital/nueva-secretaria-de- movilidad-de-bogota-deyanira-avila-moreno.

Bogota in danger: the terrifying spike in insecurity in the first half of 2023! (n/d). Gov.co. Retrieved on 13 of September 13, from 2023, from https://concejodebogota.gov.co/bogota-en-peligro-el-aterrador-repunte-de-la- inseguridad-en-el-primer/cbogota/2023-07-14/165454.php.

Regime of the civil servant regime. Retrieved on 1 of August from 2023, from http://www.esap.edu.co/portal/wp-content/uploads/2017/10/2-Regimen-del-Servidor- Publico.pdf).

WHITE PAPER on artificial intelligence - a European approach for excellence and trust Retrieved 1 August 2023, from https://eur-lex.europa.eu/legal-content/EN/TXT/PDF/?uri=CELEX:52020DC0065.

Legislation cited

Law 2213 of 2022.

Law 1755 of 2015.

Law 1581 of 2012.

Political Constitution of Colombia. Agreement 257 of 2006.
CONPES 3975-2019.

Colombian Civil Code List of abbreviations AI: Artificial Intelligence. ICT: Information and Communication Technologies. C.C: Civil Code. IDB: Inter-American Development Bank. SDM: District Mobility Secretariat.

MIX
Papier aus verantwortungsvollen Quellen
Paper from responsible sources
FSC® C105338

Printed by Books on Demand GmbH, Norderstedt / Germany